# GLUTEN INTOLERANCE

Caitie McAneney

New York

Published in 2015 by The Rosen Publishing Group, Inc.
29 East 21st Street, New York, NY 10010

First Edition

Editor: Caitie McAneney
Book Design: Mickey Harmon

Photo Credits: Cover (series logo) Alhovik/Shutterstock.com; cover (banner) moham'ed/Shutterstock.com; cover (image) Michal Kowalski/Shutterstock.com; p. 4 ChameleonsEye/Shutterstock.com; pp. 5, 13, 21 Monkey Business Images/Shutterstock.com; p. 7 Scorpp/Shutterstock.com; p. 9 Maya Kruchankova/Shutterstock.com; p. 11 (main) wavebreakmedia/Shutterstock.com; p. 11 (inset) MedicalRF.com/Getty Images; p. 15 b7/Shutterstock.com; p. 16 Africa Studio/Shutterstock.com; p. 17 Steve Cukrov/Shutterstock.com; p. 19 Blend Images - Jose Luis Palaez Inc./Brand X Pictures/Getty Images; p. 22 Sergey Novikov/Shutterstock.com.

Library of Congress Cataloging-in-Publication Data

McAneney, Caitlin.
 Gluten intolerance / Caitie McAneney.
    pages cm. — (Let's talk about it)
 Includes index.
 ISBN 978-1-4777-5790-1 (pbk.)
 ISBN 978-1-4777-5788-8 (6 pack)
 ISBN 978-1-4777-5789-5 (library binding)
 1. Celiac disease—Popular works. 2. Gluten—Health aspects—Popular works. I. Title.
 RC862.C44M33 2015
 616.3'99—dc23
                          2014028151

Manufactured in the United States of America

CPSIA Compliance Information: Batch #CW15PK: For Further Information contact Rosen Publishing, New York, New York at 1-800-237-9932

# CONTENTS

# WHAT IS GLUTEN INTOLERANCE?

Do you know what gluten is? It's a **protein** found in grains such as wheat and rye. Some people aren't able to eat gluten because their body **reacts** badly to it. These people are said to be gluten **intolerant**.

Living with gluten intolerance isn't easy. People who have it need to avoid gluten, which is found in many foods you eat every day, especially breads. Gluten is also found in many treats, such as cake and cookies.

GLUTEN FREE

People with gluten intolerance have to eat gluten-free foods. Luckily, you can buy gluten-free foods in many stores.

# INTOLERANCE, DISEASE, OR ALLERGY?

"Gluten intolerance" is a term that's used to describe both a regular food intolerance and celiac disease. Both are centered around the **digestive system**. Someone with food intolerance feels sick after eating a certain food, such as gluten. This sickness usually goes away within hours or days.

## TELL ME MORE

Gluten is found in all wheat products and also in other products. If you only feel a reaction to wheat products, you might have a wheat **allergy**.

For people with celiac disease, eating gluten can lead to more serious damage, or harm. Celiac disease is a disease, or illness, of the **immune system**. With celiac disease, the immune system attacks gluten in the body, harming the **small intestine**.

Some people mistake a wheat allergy for gluten intolerance. But a wheat allergy is an allergic reaction to wheat, not gluten.

# SYMPTOMS

Gluten intolerance and celiac disease are very serious. You can tell if you have them by watching for signs, or symptoms, after you've eaten something that has gluten in it.

Some people with gluten intolerance get symptoms that feel like the stomach flu. They may have a stomachache, gas, and **diarrhea**. People with celiac disease have these symptoms, but they might also lose weight and develop anemia over time. Anemia is a blood illness that causes tiredness and pale skin.

## TELL ME MORE

What are wheat allergy symptoms? A wheat allergy can cause an allergic reaction, such as hives, trouble breathing, stomachache, throwing up, diarrhea, and swelling of the mouth and throat.

Regular gluten intolerance symptoms go away with time. With celiac disease, a reaction to gluten causes damage that lasts.

# WHAT HAPPENS?

What happens to someone who has celiac disease if they eat gluten? Their immune system attacks the villi (VIH-ly) on the inside of the small intestine. This causes the villi to swell and become damaged.

Villi are little fingerlike parts that line the small intestine and take in **nutrients** from food. It's very important that villi get enough nutrients from food in order to keep someone healthy. When someone's immune system attacks villi, it can cause damage that sometimes can't be fixed.

## TELL ME MORE

Celiac disease is often passed down through families. If someone in your family has celiac disease, you're more likely to have it.

**villi**

Someone with celiac disease might not get enough nutrients from food if their villi are damaged from eating gluten.

# AVOIDING GLUTEN

If you think you have gluten intolerance, it's important to go to a doctor to find out. A doctor can test your blood and sometimes a piece of your small intestine. If you have gluten intolerance or celiac disease, there's only one way to avoid a reaction—don't eat gluten.

Foods with gluten include wheat, rye, and barley. These are found in breads, cereals, crackers, pasta, and fried food. Other foods—even hot dogs, sauce, and soup—may contain gluten.

## TELL ME MORE

It can be hard to remember all the foods that contain gluten. Your doctor and parents can help you make a list of food that's okay to eat and food you should avoid.

You can look on food labels to see if a canned or packaged food is gluten-free. It's best to only eat food with a gluten-free label.

# SAFE FOODS

When you have gluten intolerance, you may feel as if almost all foods are off limits. But that's not true! Safe foods include fresh fruits, vegetables, and meat. Milk, eggs, and juice are safe, too. You can also eat things made with safe grains and gluten-free flour. These include rice, soy, corn, potato, and flax.

## TELL ME MORE

You can learn more about eating gluten-free by meeting with a dietitian. Dietitians know all about food and can tell you which foods will keep you healthy and which will make you sick.

Even if you're gluten intolerant, there are many foods you can eat to stay healthy and get the nutrients you need.

If you miss eating cake or bread, don't worry! Many grocery stores and bakeries offer gluten-free foods. They even sell gluten-free cake mixes!

# WATCH OUT!

You may avoid eating foods with gluten, but watch out for contamination! That's when a food touches another food that you're not supposed to eat. People with celiac disease need to be extra careful about gluten contamination.

## TELL ME MORE

If you have celiac disease, you can help your small intestine heal itself by eating healthy, gluten-free foods. If you do eat gluten, it can cause more damage.

How can you be safe? You should use kitchen tools and a cooking space that are very clean or aren't used for gluten. That means you might have your own toaster so bits of bread don't contaminate your food.

It's good to keep your gluten-free food away from other food in your kitchen. It's also important to not share food with your friends!

# SPEAK UP

You may feel uncomfortable telling people you can't eat gluten. However, it's very important to speak up about it. Your teachers, friends, and family want you to stay healthy!

If you're gluten intolerant, you may need to eat different food than the rest of your class. You also need to speak up when you're at restaurants. Tell the waiter you need only gluten-free food and it can't be contaminated.

You can bring safe food from home so you don't feel left out at lunch or snack time.

# FRIENDS HELPING OUT

Maybe you don't have gluten intolerance, but you know someone who does. Maybe it's a classmate, family member, or friend. How can you help them?

First, you can help keep them safe by not sharing your food with them. Your food might have gluten in it or might have been contaminated with gluten. If you're bringing treats to school, bring a special gluten-free treat for your friend. Make sure to keep it separate from the other treats.

> The best thing you can do for your friend is to make them feel accepted. Let them know you understand their gluten intolerance and will help any way you can!

# NOT ALONE

If you have gluten intolerance, you may feel left out. You may be the only one in your class who has it. But you're not alone! Over 2 million people in the United States have celiac disease, and even more have regular gluten intolerance.

Unfortunately, there's no cure for gluten intolerance yet. The best thing you can do is stay positive about living a gluten-free life. Discover all the yummy gluten-free foods that are safe to eat!

# GLOSSARY

**allergy:** A bad immune system reaction to certain foods, animals, or surroundings.

**diarrhea:** Very soft or runny solid waste from a person or animal.

**digestive system:** The system of body parts that helps turn the food you eat into the power your body needs.

**immune system:** The system that keeps the body safe from sicknesses.

**intolerant:** Unable to accept a certain food.

**nutrient:** Something taken in by a plant or animal that helps them grow and stay healthy.

**protein:** Matter supplied by food that helps build and repair tissues in the body.

**react:** To do something because of something else.

**small intestine:** A long tube of tissue where food is broken down to be taken into the blood.

# INDEX

# WEBSITES

Due to the changing nature of Internet links, PowerKids Press has developed an online list of websites related to the subject of this book. This site is updated regularly. Please use this link to access the list: www.powerkidslinks.com/ltai/glut